REBEL EYES

Poetry, Prose and Short Stories

3rd Revision

DMITRY WILD

REBEL EYES

Poetry, Prose and Short Stories

Credits:
Cover Art by Artem Mirolevich
Back Photo by Anna Azarov
Book Design by Say Wow Media

Chapter Art:
Page 13 - Art by Igor Molochevski
Page 25 - Photo by Jenniffer Claroscura
Page 43 - Art by Artem Mirolevich
Page 67 - Art by Yana Fox
Page 93 - Painting by Dmitry Wild
Page 109 - Solomon's Seal (Artist Unknown)
Page 134 - Stock Photo
Page 155 - Photo by Jenniffer Claroscura

Thank You to my friends for
sharing their art and time for the
sake of this book.

Dear Reader

Here I have collected poems, prose and short stories from when I was a rebel youth running around the Lower East Side in New York, looking for the meaning of life at the bottom of the bottle, in cigarette's dim light, at the end of the night, in stranger's eyes, discovering depth and darkness, exploring rebellion and sex, and then finding love and becoming a father. Conversations, free-form streams of consciousness, convoluted stories, observations or simple moments of wonder are seared on those pages.

—Dmitry Wild

Contents

CHAPTER 4
WILD LOVE

CHAPTER 5
ABSTRACT MINUETS

CHAPTER 6
EXISTENTIAL WONDERING

108

CHAPTER 7
MIRROR REFLECTIONS

134

CHAPTER 8
THE LIGHT OF FATHERHOOD
154

IMMIGRANT'S

WINDOW

Unless you have been an immigrant yourself, you wouldn't know what's it like to be an immigrant in a new land, new language, no friends, no perspective

It's good when you have a family, but if you don't it gets worse. You feel like the loneliest dog on the street. You want to howl from misery of not having your own bone to suck on.

If you move within the same country, at least people speak the same language, they have some similarities, but when everything is new it's shocking. It feels as if you are a baby and you have to grow up again.

Our choice is what shapes us, but sometimes your family makes the choices for you especially if you are little teenager with big plans so you stare outside of your window thinking of that faraway distant land and tear rolls down your face.

Russia

How many bells she made
that tolled to enemies arriving
How many men she blinded
with her heavenly and yellow light
Just like the mother that leaves her child
in the middle of the river
that carried him towards his life's delight

How many tears she shed
rolling down the hills and birches
How many times she died
inside the golden churches
No, I won't ask her for forgiveness,
but when I am walking
I still hear bells on
quiet winter nights

Creamy water

I have slept on the asphalt
of New York City

I have seen the sunset
over the red rocks in Sedona

I have seen the waves of the
Pacific Ocean on Route One in California

I walked up and down
the streets of New Orleans

I camped and ran from a bear in
the woods of New Mexico

I sat in a Jacuzzi overlooking the
Great Smoky Mountains

I saw the Cherokee Indians of
South Carolina rub history
lessons back in white men's faces

I have seen the endless horizon
of the Mojave Desert

I have been to Elvis's house in
Memphis

and drank my whiskey
in Nashville

I swam in the blue waters
of the Caribbean Islands

I climbed the magnificent
Machu Pichu and played
music on the streets of Lima

I drank wine in Rome and danced at
Festival of masks in Venice

I smelled the rain of old England
and ate the best Fish and Chips

and all those things you can do too,
but only I know
how water tastes in the lake
next to the country house where I grew up

108th Street Rap

Babushkis are nesting
on the corner streets
Listening to Russian radios
 they're feeling homesick
Limo drivers buy piroshkies
 at the magazines
Flashing their gold jewelry
to the deli Sikhs.

"Покупай, Покупай"
Bro you got a bimmer?
There is my brand new Mercedes-Benz
I got techno blasting from the
tinted windows man

There is a hot Bukharian Chick
in my back seat
I just bought her
an Engagement 24Karat Ring

My uncle is Dentist,
my bro sells Real Estate
He demolishes old homes
and builds palaces instead

We all live on 108th street
It's our refuge, it's our bliss
We are the kings of 108th street
Don't you try to even dis

We're friends

We are tied by unknown strings
We sit at Russian Bath houses
We create designs for art
We work on Shakespeare novels
and talk of women as statues of erotic art
and slap each other on the backs when we laugh
at a joke so well understood

We laugh and down the shots
with some mind bending alcohol inside
We eat caviar and curse profoundly
and smoke and powder our noses
with long lines of white esthetic cosmic powders
Proclaiming our eternal love for each other
 and how glad we are that we have met

But when it's business time
with razor edge eyes we evaluate each other's
worth and measuring the weight of every word and
slicing the silence of the moment with a knife
before we make a decision
on how much money we can invest
to be the new immigrant kings of New York

I am sure tomorrow we will get a drink together,
but today the leftover of the evening still lingers
from my newly founded friends and a sharp piece of mirror
is stuck in my heart somewhere deep inside.

Mother's Love

While you are far away
I am building my ships here
but when we talk
your love overwhelms me

I am your son
and always will be
and you will always be
my earth family

In love I was born and
love I will create all around
Since the day you brought me up
under this big white sky,
but stop calling me every
other day and asking me why?

Why didn't I call?
Do I not love you anymore?
Did I forget I have parents?
Ma come on,
you know I love you
☺

Ночь

Мы выехали ночью
когда было темно
Заползли усталые
через гряазное окно

Перегруженный город
остался позади
В глаза нам залетали
красные огни

Мы ехали по пыльным
и лесным дорогам
Река убегала
за каменным забором

От передозы становилось
уже все равно
Мы засыпали и курили,
не открывая окно

Мы лежали на дороге
и гуляли по деревьям
Мы летали по поляне и
бегали по звездам
Нам было хорошо,
мы танцевали сидя
В ту ночь мы знали что-то
и радовались тихо

Night

(Translated from Russian)

We drove out at night
When it was dark
Tired crawled inside
Through the dirty window

Overstuffed city
was left behind
Red Lights glided
 into our eyes

We drove down the dusty
and the forest roads
River was running away
under the stone fence

We stopped caring
from the overdose
We fell asleep and smoked
without opening car windows

We laid on the roads
and walked on the trees
We flew over the fields
and we ran over the stars

We felt so alive
We danced sitting down

that night we knew something
and we were quietly blessed

WILD

YOUTH

Youth is such a beautiful and raw time.
It's the time when you feel anything can happen
to you.

Everything could work.
You burn and burn through the days and nights.
Full of passion for people, books, conversations,
late nights, getting stoned, drunk or just happy.

You just are, floating aimlessly getting high on
a new album, book, song or movement. Trying
to always get to the next best thing. Smoking
those endless cigarettes and finishing those end-
less alcohol bottles so you can end up at the same
kitchen again, being wasted asking your friends
that you love so much, so what's the plan for
tonight, shall we get high at home or let's go out
and see what's out there?!

But also there is that thing called being melan-
cholic for the youth that's leaving and what's
coming to you is a beast of by the name of
adulthood.

Kitchen Talks with Jesus

Cocaine. Oh how I loved Cocaine. I could think clearly, enjoy music, connect to people of all walks of life on some basic life loving level. Feeling the taste of dirt in my throat was satisfying. It reminded you of the fact that you did something special. Illegal. My one problem with it was that it always ended. I had an un-manifested desire every time I did it to have an unlimited supply. Every time I stared at the empty bag I dreamed that one day I could have as much cocaine as I wanted. Felix was an acquaintance of ours. He was the type of short Latin guy that you meet a lot in the city, only he spoke English really well. Felix looked kind of normal. A bit of grey hair, jeans, shirt, jacket. Only there was something radiating from him, something that spoke louder than words. He was also a cokehead.

We had a few drinks and did a few lines in the bathroom together, then since you always have to be extra careful he said let's go to my house to continue the party. We picked up a six pack and all three of us went to his house.

Once we got to his house, he said his friend was going to come over. In about 20 minutes, another Latin looking guy came in, he was tall wore denim jeans and had a slick back hair and a cigarette sticking out of his mouth. He dropped a plastic bag on the table. He said, "Hi, Guys, Felix told me he was bringing some friends over so I got us a little 'something special' for the evening. That's for us!" It was a plastic grocery bag, the type they use in convenience stores, with more than a quarter full of cocaine. Felix introduced us. His name was Jesus. I smiled…

It's 3 am. This decadent old apartment had pale kitchen wallpaper, with rips here and there. White fridge, a giant manifestation of an old world, and the table's plastic cloth had squares on it. In the middle of the table laid a round mirror. On the surface of the mirror there are 4 long and thick lines of cocaine. Next to it is a white grocery plastic bag with more cocaine. We have been at it since 10pm in the evening, but we didn't care anymore. We are talking with Jesus. Each one of us took a short straw and snorted a line every 15 minutes.

We are discussing our neighbor in Queens or more like we are complaining to Jesus. We are telling him of the events that occurred last night. Our neighbor upstairs blasts middle eastern music all through the night and screams over it in a loud hysterical voice. He doesn't let us sleep. In the morning we called the noise complaint hotline, not sure what they could do, but it was literally a nightmare.

Jesus responded after snorting another line, "Let him be, and say thank God you are not in his place."

We were dumbfounded and started to protest, "But… He is crazy… We can't live like this."

He said, "Leave him alone and that's that!"

We disagreed in silence, and he continued, "Maybe he is a God, Dionysus himself, or a bull before the toreador, his maker. Maybe his screams ripping through his throat, accompanied by the sound coming from the speakers are the sound of his agony. Maybe it's the sound of a caged animal, him being misunderstood, slowly killed. Maybe he is terminally ill. Let the crazy music rip through the night and let one more soul be at peace, while you should find another place to live."

We nodded in understanding, agreeing that we haven't looked at it from that angle.

We talked about a lot of stuff with Jesus and his friend Felix. At some point the door buzzer went off. Felix gets up and opens the door. Another Hispanic guy walks in, the type you see working at the back of the grocery store or as a cook at the kitchen. He was holding a plastic cup with booze inside and by the looks of him, he'd started few hours ago. Felix looks at him and says, "Amigo, que paso?" Meanwhile Felix turns around to us and says quietly that it's his neighbor, Jose, and that he usually never drinks, something must have happened. I decide to play Jesus and after introducing myself and my girl I start asking him questions. How is he doing? We find out that his wife is about to go to the hospital, and he doesn't know why. They are about to take her away and he doesn't know what else to do except make himself drunk until he is happy. I was questioning him, what happened before? Was there anything unusual about her or their situation? He stared at the floor for a while and then guiltily said, "Well, she think I cheat man." We all exclaimed, "Are you?" and he answered, "No man, she is just my amiga. We are friends, but my esposa gets jealous." I ask him, "When was the last time you took your wife on a date?" He answered looking down again, "I don't know we got kids you know." I sat down lit a cigarette and said, "I am not a doctor, but I think if you go back to your wife and tell her you love her, and that there is no other woman but her, her health just might improve and she might not have to go to the hospital." He looked at me, "You think so?" I said, "What have you got to lose? Try it. If no one knows the reason for her illness, maybe there is no illness. Heart break can have symptoms just like an illness, but the cure is within her heart." He put his glass down and said, "Ok amigos. I go. I tell her, she is my mujer man." I said, "Go, don't waste time." He left and as the door slammed behind him, I sat down. It felt good being Jesus for a moment, and I snorted another line. Jesus looked at me and said, "See, that wasn't too difficult. All you did was be compassionate and feel his pain and the solution was right in front of you." I was proud of myself. I looked at my girl, and grabbed her hand. She smiled and said, "You did good." We kissed. I tasted cocaine on her lips.

As the conversation progressed we found out that Jesus and Felix were high end fashion photographers. What an irony! Someone named Jesus was a fashion photographer in modern times. I guess when you are named Jesus your responsibility to the world is to help people in need or, in my case, with fulfilling their deepest desires. I just finished reading Bulgakov's literary masterpiece, Master and Margarita and I remembered that before Pontius Pilate condemned Jesus to the cross, Pontius was suffering from bad migraines. No one knew about that and he didn't tell anyone, but Jesus knew. So he asked him, "Brother take a walk with me and I will cure your headaches and reveal to you the secret of this world. "Of course the Roman prefect of Judea declined Jesus's request, claiming that nothing can cure his headache. Deep inside Pontius Pilate hated Jerusalem, hated his post and would have given anything to alleviate the suffering, since the only creature he could trust in this world was his dog.

Scene taken from the finale of the book by M. Bulgakov, *Master and Margarita* (forbidden in Russia by Communists): Satan and his close associates, the old knight, the cat and Azzazelo were galloping towards the moon on black stallions. Behind them roped by passion and love were their new friends, the eternal lovers, artist and his muse, Master and Margarita. Finally, they ascend to the moon and witness Pontius Pilate sitting on his Roman throne in Judea deep in thought, with his trusty dog by his side. Satan turns around to Master and screams, "Master finish your novel now!"

At those words, Master yells, "You are free!" At those words, Roman prefect of Judea, executioner of Jesus of Nazareth, gets up and starts walking with his dog towards the moon. There he sees Jesus ahead, with the moon radiating behind him, his arms stretched out, welcoming Pontius to take that long awaited walk.

As they slowly walk up, Pontius Pilate asks him, "Could I have jeopardized my career and post in Jerusalem to save you?" Jesus didn't reply and just looked at him with a beautiful face of serenity and acceptance and Pontius answered his own question, "Yes, I could have."

And they walked and talked and talked for centuries. It was light out. We walked outside having said our goodbyes to Felix and Jesus. We were holding on to the pole next to the subway not knowing if we were going to die now or later. My head was pounding, my jaw and my nose were numb. My girl's face was pale since she was in the same horrific predicament. We vowed to never do cocaine again. Jesus' serene face appeared in my mind.

My deepest desire was fulfilled, I got that bag of cocaine that never ended.
Thank You Jesus.

***

Burning Stars

My trees are taller than your lies
My days last longer than your wine
My words are windows to the skies
that I have built for you and I

Wild music always in the flow
It's my companion on the road
It could be strange enough for you,
but it's contains the hidden truth

I smoke and talk of burning stars
I am spitting fire at their farce
They never seemed to understand
that children never ever plan.

Concert in the Park

Music flies from their fingers
into the big black speakers and
then into our reluctant ears
The sea of sounds, emotions, caresses
Exploding inside,
intensely we soar among the dead,
like a wolf and a prey
Between the rugs and carpets,
pirouettes lifted, dropped, lost forever

Mozart floats above in the sky,
smiling like a mischievous child
The orchestra plays what was destined
to be alive, forever alive
His wing curls, the rippled clouds,
his soft hair unfolds like a veil
In the cloud floats the devil face,
for every brilliance you have to pay

Chuang Tzu floats behind him,
smiling like an childish sage
Half of him is an old man;
the other half is a young samurai

Fireworks, colored stars
detonate visions in our eyes
Truth told and untold
Roman theatre masks,

all pass by to come back again
some other time perhaps

But Nazis with megaphones
will not let me enjoy leftovers
of this beautiful psychedelic show

"GO HOME, PARK IS CLOSED"

I yell back.
"THIS IS MY HOME!
MY BABYLON!
F*** YOU LITTLE MAN IN BLUE SUIT,
WE ALL DO WHAT WE THINK
IS BEST"

Dancer in the Dark

Am I the dancer in the dark
Or darkness is the dancer?

One more child will lead the rest
born in the forest in the night
One more man will walk the path
learning from the divine light

Best dreams slowly start to bleed
bruises make you learn their tricks
Spy on your hand turn to fist
watch your wings grow underneath

Mount the chariot and ride
through the holes into the sky
Avant-garde is mixed with blood
We are dogs who love mistrust

Asphalt Door

The end of the careless time
Beginning of a serious life
Chase your dreams while you can
We live in between four transparent walls
We travel with books
it's two thousand four
The rules are always the same
someone stays and someone goes
Breathe it in and let it out
I am from the other side
Across the ocean I used to live,
but now, I am looking for my door
on the asphalt floor

Desert Trippers

Eyes are glowing
Movements flowing
Just like rivers
we're the desert trippers

Losing all senses
evil caresses
Music from speakers
kisses the seekers

Fires are burning
Moon is yearning
Stars under water
for sons and daughters

Eyes are expanding
Darkness is tempting
Turn off your lighters
No earthly desires

Am I the Satan yet?

Her claws and
blood marks on my arm
I love thyself like a God
acting out his greatest love

Head bashed in with a cross of fire
Red curtains over my face
"Welcome to the family,"
they say
What a sign!
Am I a Satan yet?

Cosmic Christ

I kissed the abundance
of her golden painted lips
I kissed the malevolent
musician on her cheeks
She welcomed and submitted
 to her vice but I could see love inside
through the painted holes for the eyes

The cosmic Christ takes pleasure
with the mother of the earth,
His sperm impregnates the
blue sky around her womb
Milky clouds are born around
the crater of our minds
We convulse, collapse and
pant until the day turns to night

I am the black bird caged in a cell
My beak is long and here, I feel at home

Beautiful people

Beautiful people
In this crazy city
Always on the run,
never see the sun

So many choices
solutions and plans
So many people
running to their den

Songs are waiting for us
women dancing for us
on top of dirty bars
Monday is also waiting for us

City of the Ghosts

Riding on a highway
in high-tech airplanes
to the city with no past
and a needle in the heart

Clouds rest on top
moon drowned in her light
I paint the outlines of
those medieval nights

My friend is on the left
he lives with a devil in disguise
They share a black panther
one in bed and one in dreams

And now we are driving slowly
to the moist and lustful words
We are driving to the center
in the city of the ghosts

All of a sudden we observe
two misty blue elevator shafts
That pierce the cloudy skies
and names of the innocent ones
are written on the silver stars
They are slowly floating inside
and dancing to our surprise
all the way into the skies

REBEL

EYES

Rebellion is part of our psyche. We can't live in acceptance of everything all the time. Human beings are not made to be governed by the old ideals and other people whose intent is not making us grow spiritually and intellectually. The only type of governing should happen when we need knowledge, otherwise human beings are free to do and think as they wish. One cannot say follow my dogma and if you don't do it, I will kill you. Naturally, he will become a dictator. Yes, he can kill one, two, ten, one hundred, one thousand, perhaps even a million, but there will be more people who will stand up and throw his rule off their shoulders and declare themselves free men. You can witness this everywhere, since the birth of humanity. Moses who led the Israelites for 40 years away from Egypt to find their new home, Alexander the Great, who captured and destroyed Persians, who were destroying Greeks and Macedonians before, French Revolution, Russian Revolution, World War 1, World War 2, Americans fighting the British yoke as a new colony, North and South fighting each other over slavery.

Humanity grows through conflict and through our inner desire and birth right to be free. Famous phrase comes to mind, "It's better to die free, than live in slavery."

Although what happens then we all know, human beings are not developed spiritually enough to withstand from the alluring power of control over other people and therefore. Those that promise us the great life turn into new despots and new dictators. They come with their new dogmas and then again, the revolt is uprising. Take French Revolution which created Robespierre and the Age of Terror. Take Russian Revolution and reign of communism and those situations, are everywhere. Every new politician that will promise us the world will end up at best a lie, or at worst turn into a dictator, but what keeps this world going is our simple desire to be free. It's in our DNA in our blood and before we will become free, the way we truly want and desire it, many cataclysms will come and catastrophes, but humanity will live on fighting for their simple will to be free.

Revolution Manifesto
or conversation with thyself
at the voting booth

Oh revolution,
Such a sweet dame
that joins us in smoky French cafes
She wears a veil and exposes
one breast for us to suck on
Artists, poets, romantics,
vagabonds and mainly
idealists at heart
love such a burlesque show

She is like a goddess of
most primal nature
She lifts her skirt
and then she ravages
her bayonet into your groin
"Remember your birthright,"
she says, "You are free!"

It's that notion of being free
To do what?
To do what we want to do?
What is it that we want to do?
We want to be free to do
what we want to do!

Young hearts chant with their fists up in the air,
"We will no longer put up with such a treatment.
Corporations are all greedy mongrels.
Their knives are at our throats
Let's take away from the rich
and give to the poor!"

Ok let's!

Let's take France,
Paris and La Marseillaise,
What noble symbols
and such laurels!
Now think of what followed,
the grand butcher, Robespierre
and the Reign of Terror

I, myself, hail from the land of
Grande Communism,
The bloody Russia
where such slogans won the war
and equalized everyone to zero
Demolished everything that
Peter the Great earned with sweat and tears
They again stained the land
with blood of rich
and poor and angry became the Red Commissars
whose plight was far from grim

What did they do with all the stolen goods?
Well, they became the rich again
Veiled under the red flag they filled their coffers
and removed the heads of those whose eyes
witnessed what they had done
Under the pretense of treason

Can we really govern ourselves?
Can those in control rule with their hearts?
Can people really live in peace?
Can people really live in harmony?

We are not ready; we are still beasts!
They say the purest state of mind and happiness that
anyone can remember is when we were kids

That eternal drifting
on the surface of the world,
Such bliss to have no cares,
but have you forgotten
your first lesson?
The first fight on the playground?

Babies don't even verbalize their
needs, but they already tug on each other's
toys cries resembling yells,
"I like yours more than mine!
Give me what you have!
Give me! Give me!
I don't want to play with my toy anymore! "

How can we be at peace?
when at the core of our
existence we compare what we have
to someone else's affairs all the time?

Let's suppose for argument's sake we have nothing
We have no possessions.
We live in a garden,
an Eden's garden
and we see an apple
and another homo sapient over there
found a more beautiful apple.

That's it!
The end of peace!
Our want is gnawing on our mind,
like a hungry dog gnaws on a bone

Now it's freedom
then it's choices
then it's respect
then it's something else

We strive for what
we can't have at the moment
If only we realized
we have so much right now
All we need is within us now
All we need is inside us now
Humanity is a zoo

Animal is happiest alone
without their brother or sisters
scowling at his food

Peace is within and
revolution is with oneself
Try to win that one
Every day you have a chance
No need to seek it
Inwards your eyes
First, we must conquer ourselves
and then, yell it to the world!

I still vote for change,
I always will
We need to believe in change
that's what makes fear disappear
because I believe that only change will get us there,
but let's not call it revolution,
let's call it transformation,
evolution or may be regeneration,
but we all wish for the same
to get there
wherever and whatever
THERE
is.

Alexander the Great

Father says: "Now you know
How it feels to kill another soul
How the vultures eat your liver
For giving fire to the people!"

Saw his destiny from birth
fought greatest battles on this earth
Where the mother laid with snakes
sending father far from grace

Conquering unknown worlds
guided by a winged bird
aimed his sword up at the sky
and ignited people's eyes

Conquered fear and death
Raising the cities behind
he knew wild women and men,
He screamed,
"RIDE MACEDONIANS! RIDE!"

TV lies

Watch watch watch
What they show show show
Have have have
what you see, see see

Do, do, do
as they tell, telltale
walk, walk, walk
where they say, say, say

Can't you hear hear hear
how they preach, teach, lynch
They destroy, troy, troy
if you are weak, sick, tricked

If you see, see, see
Through the screen, scream, dream
Come to us, us, us
We are your TV lies, lies, lies

Dead Electricity

Walking through the dark city
observing the empty streets
People are sleeping in fear
may be the chaos is near

Searching for liquid supply
we are going to get so high
We're going to dance tonight
We're gonna go back in time

The darkness defeated the light
feels like seventeen seventy-nine
Moon and the stars in the sky
are the only gods of the light?

Everybody seemed to forget
everybody can't understand
what to do with themselves
when the electricity is dead

Fear Mantra

Fear does not own me
Fear does not control me

I was born thousands of years ago
When transparent souls roamed
the sea
and there was nothing but
pure consciousness and will

I had to fight the fear of birth
through the thunderous rain
Born to a mother in a cave
with pieces of animal skin
she covered me up
as I suckled on her breasts

I had to light my first fire
and to kill my first meal
I praised that animal
for letting me live
since it died for me
to keep on living

I accepted fear as a real being and
It only made me stronger
It ran through me like
a midnight runner
but it didn't linger

It dissolved into an ocean
like the sand castle turns back into the sand

I wore the armor
of the Macedonian soldier,
who laughed in the face of fear
holding up my javelin
like a torch in the times of darkness

I was there in the Inquisition era
screaming out to the crowds,
"My name is Mennochio
There is nothing to fear
Our god doesn't want you to fear him!
He wants you to love this world
and to love thyself!
That church is not his house,
but of his fanatic prophets."

The sin was their advertising campaign
Oh yeah they worked it well into our brain
They dragged me down
tied to the pole,
but my tongue was untied
As I looked at the flames around me
they burned me as I was saying,
"God is the air that we breathe!"

They used fear
to enslave people's minds

They used Nietzsche's ideas
to create superior race
I was there when the tank was rolling over me
I threw a grenade into that
Panther's engine
Fear was in their eyes not in mine,
I was fighting for my country

We knew no fear as we fought and liberated European
cities:
Poland, Romania, Belgrade, Paris and Germany,
We got up when our friends
were down
I died many times but
kept on running forward
I was there when we put up
our flag on top of Reichstag

Fear is the greatest thief
of the universal ignorance bliss
Dressed in the overcoat
with a Tommy gun underneath
Riding on men's backs
robbing them of happiness
and satisfaction

If you let it!
If you let it!
Do you let it?
Or you let it be?

I choose to be free of
fear and doubt
Silver string leads me
to the body in the realm of
consciousness and sound
I choose to be free from
Fear and Doubt!
Soul and Body in the realm
of consciousness and sound!

Fear doesn't not own me
Fear doesn't control me

Naked and Fearless
I will turn into consciousness
ethereal and ever-present
Manifestation of the Great Krishna
I create my own lucid dream world and
my intellect is my library of knowledge

Knowledge sticks a knife
in the heart of fear
The more you know the less you fear
The more you know the less you fear
The more you know the less you fear
The more you know the less you fear

Fear does not own me
Fear does not control me

I am free from fear and doubt
I left go and I let God

I dreamt of my baby today
I held him in my hands as I gave him his first lesson:
"Do not fear, you are a lion cub!"

1800FLOWERS.com

Fans of American football are selling flowers
Women's holiday is a commercial plot
Workers say,
"I hate Valentine's Day!
I can't take it anymore!
I can't sell any more flowers!"

Do women know that Valentine's Day is the 2nd of
the best-selling and profitable holidays in the chart of
generating the most revenue?
1st holiday is Christmas.

Men are searching on the web
for gifts for their women
Spiders on mars are also searching
for gifts to satisfy their spider women

What a woman really wants is
to laugh, to hear some poetry,
a little understanding and
hot and sweaty night of sex!

4 Times Square

I landed into the beast's overcoat
into the number 4 of his 6 arms.
The allies on the right,
those who own their shadow come from the left
The beast unveiled himself before me
in all its glory and golden mass
The buzzing, screaming, honking,
flashing, and tourist trash

Everything moves along his veins
with the sole purpose - to succeed
To conquer stomach, eyes, the mind
and ears is the science of the beast
To make the winner step over the loser,
to be at the head of this procession
Carrying the gifts of sacrifice, of hate,
of lust, of fame of whoredom

His huge and pumping belly
is full of glowing lights
Broadway shows, slogans and
the goddesses of fashion

The billboards sell public saints
who exhibit their shiny teeth
and their smiles are ever faint

And I will join them, oh yes and

I will be the best among the rest
'cause now I feel
as if the time has come
for the true artist
to become a man

To set a gun pointing
at my own consciousness
and set the trigger on slow motion
as it all comes down...

Ok my lunch is over,
gotta go back up to work now.

Рыцари

Идут рыцари, бренчат доспехами
не мониторами и не мышками
а шпорами об камни мостовой
идут и вспоминают вчерашний бой

Идут покинув головы на грудь
Кто остался позади их не вернуть
Кто рядом был теперь их нет
теперь им не увидеть белый свет

Они сражались за имя короля
а девы на берегу реки стоят
последнюю им песню распевают
их голоса любимых не достигают

И когда последний звук затихнет
они с обрыва упадут как слезы матери великой
которая плачет а сыне который ускакал с мечом
и не вернется больше никогда в родимый дом

Я берусь за мышку и выключаю
Netflix ну а потом и монитор

Мда, им было жить не легко
А я завтра не пойду на работу
Буду лежать и ничего не делать
И радоваться что можно пить вино
Надо еще какой то девчонке позвонить,
а то одному грустно вино пить

Knights

(Translated from Russian)

Knights are walking, their armor is clanking
Not computer monitors or computer mouse
but their spurs are clanking on the pavement
They are walking and
  reminiscing about yesterday's battle

They are walking with their heads on their chests
Who was left behind they can't return them back
Who was next to them now they are no more
Now they won't see the big white light anymore

They fought for the name of the king,
while their brides sang on the river bend
singing their parting song
The voices of their loved ones
won't reach them anymore

and when their last notes will die down
they will fall down into the river
just like the tear drops of the great mother
that cries about her lost son who
rode out on the horse with a sword and
will never return to their ancestral home

I turn off the computer mouse,
then Netflix and then my monitor,
Yeah life for them wasn't easy

but I won't go to work tomorrow,
I will lay in my bed and do nothing
and be grateful that you can drink wine
and I should call some girl
because drinking wine by yourself is a sad affair.

WILD

LOVE

How I met my bride,
the Daughter of the Moon

That particular day I was having a good time at the studio working on a new record with my current band # 7; it was a glorious Saturday in April. I was wearing my black velvet jacket and things were good, since I had just met up with my drug dealer and picked up a fresh bag of the stuff you powder your nose with to make yourself feel even more glorious.

Of course I was going to my favorite bar to get lit, I had kind of became a regular there. I precisely liked the smell of that place. As you walk in, your nostrils are filled with the smell of alcohol, toilet water, and incense sticks, a smell that appealed to me at that time - it made me feel like I was at home. As I opened the door that day the same smell filled my nostrils and I exhaled deeply anticipating a great night. There were only few people at the place and a blues record was playing, filling empty space in the room with the sound of old souls and vintage guitars. As I was walking to the bathroom to start my night I noticed a gorgeous creature sitting on a stool at the bar. I saw her profile and when she looked at me I felt the mystery of the moon itself staring back at me. She sported pitch-black long hair down her back, a red shirt, red lipstick, tight blue jeans, and black knee-high boots with stiletto heels that made you want to lick them or get your ear lobe pierced with them. What attracted me the most were her eyes. She had those eyes that made her look mystical and exotic. I felt a jolt in my heart from her beauty. I decided to talk to her when I got out of the bathroom hoping she would still be sitting there. After I closed the toilet lid I made two perfect white lines of that magic powder and inhaled them deeply with a feeling of satisfaction. I left the bathroom with an elevated spirit and a whole lot of courage, I was elated. The beautiful creature was still sitting there, so I pulled up a bar stool right next to her. She sipped her drink slowly and gave me this look that said, don't even talk to me, I can see right through your intentions.

Let me tell you, I sucked at small talk or starting a good conversation with girls. No matter how good you look, starting a conversation is a skill and an art form that one must develop, kind of like driving. I sucked at it majorly; awkward phrases would spill out of my mouth, but this time, things were different. It was a good day and the magic powder was making its way into my brain, I decided to let it flow, whatever comes out of my mouth. Nothing could go wrong.

Nevertheless, earlier that day someone had sent me an email with a list of the cheesiest pick-up lines ever used on the female population by men. She was looking at me waiting, so I threw a line from the list at her and said,

"So do you come here often or do you wait till you leave?" She tried not to smile at that one, but it was hard so she half-smiled with a corner of her mouth and then said,

"Do you know it's the worst pick up line I ever heard?" and she laughed. I thought, well, that was a good start.

I said, "I know that was the worst one and that's why I said it - to make you laugh." Somehow that started our conversation. I asked her what was she doing here and we proceeded to talk, or more like me asking her question and her responding with one-liners. I asked her what she does for a living, she said,

"I am a musician and a dreamer." I was pleasantly surprised. "Really? I am a musician, too." I continued questioning her, becoming amused and more entangled in her mysterious world. I wanted to test her a bit, so I asked her,

"How do you write your songs?"

She answered, "from the future." I was sitting there with my mouth open. It seemed that she was trying to make me go away by giving me really deep answers, thinking I would get scared, but I was only getting more and more intrigued. I thought to myself, this girl is special, meanwhile trying to make sure my jaw was not grinding too much, giving away my mischief. She wasn't sure what her tactic should be either, so she said,

"Anyways, what are you doing here talking to me? I am only going to marry an alien or the overman." I sat there and it was my turn to smile. I thanked the gods of literature who had whispered novels into writer's ears. This year I read, "Thus Spoke Zarathustra" by Nietzsche and it changed my life. It blew my mind to pieces. It made me rethink the whole society and my role in it. The writing was strong, revolutionary. I only had two options: to shoot myself or to become The Overman, (Übermensch in German) the model of a human being that Nietzsche was calling on everyone to strive towards, to go through the transformation of becoming the camel, the lion and then the child. I took Nietzsche's calling and formed a band and called it The Overman. It was a gothic band; dark, broody and poetic. I had few shows booked and earlier on I printed a stack of flyers advertising future shows. I reached into my back jean pocket, retrieved one and dropped it on the bar in front of this beautiful creature. On the flyer it read, "The Overman" playing at … Under the title loomed my tall figure dressed in black. She was stunned and she couldn't hide it. We laughed. I said triumphantly, "Now can we talk?" She smiled looking straight at me now.

I continued while I had the advantage, "What country are you from?"

She answered, "Peru." I said, "I didn't know that such a country exists." She said, "What do you mean? It's a pretty big. It's in Latin America. Haven't you heard of Machu Pichu?" I said, "No, what's that?"

She smiled, "Where are you from?"

I said, "Russia."

She answered, "Oh that's funny. I didn't know what Russia was until this one time I was watching a metal TV show and they were showing all those wild guys moshing in the crowd to Sepulture and I thought wow those guys look crazy, but they were good looking so it was interesting to watch." All of a sudden, some tall, skinny, hairy Latin guy, came up to her and asked her quickly,

"Who are you talking to?"

She snapped back,

"None of your business dude, go talk to your date over there. She is getting bored."

I looked at the young girl sitting on the bench by the wall, and noticed she was pensive, not sure what to do with herself in such situations. He exhaled annoyingly and said,

"Whatever," and walked away.

I asked, "Who was that?"

She said, "It was my husband." I said, "Really?" Things were getting interestingly complicated, I thought to myself. Then she sipped on her drink, "Well, ex-husband. We are separated, but he is dating other people."

I said, "Wow, it's kinda fucked up." But, hey, I thought, that means she is single, like me. The bar started filling up and there were more people here and there. It was starting to get loud. The DJ showed up and started spinning records so I said, "Hey you wanna dance?" Brown Sugar by the Rolling Stones was blasting through the big speakers and we started dancing. The tall Latin hairy guy kept coming up to her and grabbing her hand, that kind of bothered me, and things looked complicated, so I said, "Hey! Let's' go downstairs." We went downstairs to the bar in the basement, which resemebled a bat cave that only the chosen ones knew about. It was dark with people here and there, with the DJ spinning at the back. We found a spot on wooden benches. She seemed frustrated with that guy. I decided to change the topic, so I asked, tell me more about your country since I know nothing about it. She started telling me a story about UFOs diving in the water as she and her psychic friend were watching. I wanted to know everything about this girl, mystique and mystery were oozing from her lips like sap from a birch tree. I thought she was the most beautiful thing I ever met. So I leaned over and caught her beautiful red lips with mine. Her lips were wet and soft. I felt myself falling into a cosmic well. It was warm and stars were shining. I felt as if I was driving that UFO with her and we were diving into that cool water together. Her annoying ex-husband found us and said, "Hey, what are you doing here? That's it let's go. We gotta go home." I was pissed off at him. I was holding her hand not sure whether to start getting violent or not, and then she said, "Don't worry about him. I gotta go. We live together, and he is my only ride home, but I will see you again." I was dumbfounded, "I thought you said you guys are separated." She replied, "Yeah, we have been separated for two years already, but we live in the same house, since I have nowhere else to go. He has a car and I can't drive, so he has to drive us since we live in New Jersey." I scratched my head and said, "All right, let me walk you to the car." As we were walking to the car, I started a conversation with him and asked, "So what happened to that girl you were with." He said, "She had to go." I learned that he was also a musician and that the girl I just met and him were in the same band together. I was like, "Wow, now that's crazy."

Aside from his jerky, asshole attitude he seemed like a cool guy after all. When when we got to their car I shook his hand and said, "Hey it was nice meeting you," – then I stopped and then continued, "but it was better meeting her. Ha ha ha!" and I laughed really loud in his face, leaving them both to drive home together in this weird and complicated situation.

I walked home happy, hoping to get her away from that house and this weird dude's life and marry her and make her mine forever, which I did.

Wild Woman

My wild woman with cat eyes
and purple essence
You wear it so eloquently and so light
The way you walk above the ground
carrying so many worlds inside

Your constellations
make we wonder how you became
in touch with them?
Through thought, or through the
grace of ancient dreamers?

Sometime I think you Persian
or sometimes a Hindu goddess
with those voluptuous breasts
that adorn the walls
of the castles built for love,
full of incense smells
and air full of glory for the divine.
No, no you are something else!

We meditate together and
collision of our worlds
creates low rumbling in our universes
Somewhere above we sit
and breathe into the
silence in our hearts
until we feel expansion deep inside

and noise succumbs and then
we lay on brown floor and
you stretch and whisper,
"Read me some Rumi."
and I silently narrate the Shams

I haven't been born a painter, but
I was given words to describe
significance of things and so
I narrate your portrait on this page

Oh your thoughts,
I love them and you inner world
Have you been born up there?
On top of that distant mountain,
where no one knows
how stones were carried to
such hellish heights
Have you hidden the secret
of our galaxy inside your womb?
Your hips, they way
they carry my future child,
as if they came from
some distant dream.
I love them now
Is this a dream?

Love is a Dancer

Love is a dancer
Love is the wind
She is my mistress
She will set me free

Love makes me shiver
Love makes me cry
It is the reason
Why we are still alive

Open your windows
Take a look outside
It rains for no reason
It's love from the sky

Don't waste your words,
Take her home tonight
Make her your queen;
whisper, "You are mine!"

Don't waste your chance
Follow us outside
We don't need any reasons
The stars and the night

Girl, show him the way,
Whisper into his heart

How to make you feel all right
Make you feel fine

What saved me was
the other side of the night

Дождь

Белая птица по небу ползет
Крылья трещат в небе песок
Ветер уносит луна улетает
Люди себя не понимают

Глаза открываются шире и шире
Дни все короче а ночи длинее
Все чаше один я гуляю по крыше
Мозг мой копает поглубже пониже

Стакан дождем наполни скорее
Дождь для меня себя не жалеет
Ты улыбаешься из далека
Я не один, Ты не одна
Ты не один, Я не одна
Ча!

Rain (translation)

White bird crawls through the sky
Wings are crackling, sand in the sky
Wind blows me away, and moon flies away
People don't understand themselves

Eyes opening wider and wider
While days become shorter nights are now longer
More often I am walking on the roof by myself
My brain is digging deeper and deeper

Fill your glass quickly with rain water
Rain doesn't pity itself for my sake
You are smiling from far away
I am not alone, and you are not alone
Chaa!

God is a Woman

My god is a woman
And she is laying in my bed
She was made for loving
So I am loving her back

She picked me up
when I was laying in dirt
and now I am thankful to her
and we are not of this earth

Egyptian Dream

Today we celebrate our birthdays.
She turned Egyptian queen and I turned man
Come father of sleep
and take your son away
to the shores of river Nile

A little while ago
I gave her snakes of love
that poisoned her
and now she's lost her mind
and laying still and
moaning to the rhythm
of her heart

I saw her beauty there at last
when all the guards were down
we lost our names,
our bodies and our souls took a little walk
to the land of the everlasting desire...

Destroyer and a Giver

Mother earth performs her role
and lives in every untamed girl
That walks barefoot in the green soil

She will become the giver
and the destroyer
once she tastes
the semen on
her tongue

Did God have sex?

I love sex...

Sex is like a hurricane of the most basic nature...

I enjoy inserting my beastly phallus into her ocean
and observing her reaction...
Her giving in...
Forgetting her own name, her cheeks are flushing...

Saliva coming down my mouth...
I feel like I want to bite a piece of her neck, or her
thigh. May be I am turning into a werewolf. I don't
know why saliva always comes down from my mouth,
but I can see it falling on her back now. She doesn't
mind.

I am tense but driving it in...
I keep on driving it in...

She is panting...
Letting go...

The true artist knows the importance of sex
that's why it's essential
to our well being
It is the drug of the psyche

The climax is like an ocean wave covering us both…
The fireworks going off in our heads…
The liquid is the juice of birth…

When Memnoch, The Devil turned himself into a man
he wanted to experience a woman's womb… Once he
experienced the sexual pleasure with a rebel woman
that ran away from her tribe (Irony ?) he compared
it to be the closest thing to being in heaven, his lost
home.

That feeling of exchanging the scent of human love
was the most amazing thing that God created on earth,
he thought, but why don't they know how amazing it
feels to be a man as well as an angel in heaven?
The creator knew that the collision of the opposites
leads to birth.

That's how the matter was born…
Did God have sex?
or God is SEX?

Свобода За Стенкой
(In Russian)

За стеной трое. Два парня и голос женщины, моей соседки. Сначала они долго смеются. Наверно они выпивают или курят траву и соответсвенно им весело.

Потом смех прекращается и переходит в ее неровное дыхание. Я должен спать, но вместо этого я напряженно вслушиваюсь. Она с перерывами дышет. Два мужских голоса над ней тихо стонут. Я замираю. Потом я слышу слитое дыхание трех тел в акте совершенства. Мое сердце бьется быстрее. Это происходит так рядом со мной, как будто я с ними за стенкой.

Они продолжают заниматься дикой любовью на протяжении дватцати минут. Акт полной свободы, разрывающий все нити нормального. Они втроем, свобода и наслаждение. Они живут и дышат друг другом. Они существуют в этом желании. Она вдруг начинает стонать громче. Какой красивий полёт, моё сердце открылось.

Жена поворачивается ко мне и говорит, "Наша соседка она такая шлюха."

Freedom behind the wall.
(Translated to English)

There are three behind the wall. Two guys and the voice of the woman, my neighbor. At first they laugh for a long time. Probably they drink or smoke grass and everything is fun for them.

Then the laughter ceases and passes into her uneven breath. I have to sleep, but instead I'm listening intently. She breathes intermittently. Two male voices above her quietly moan. I freeze. Then I hear the fusion of three bodies in the act of perfection. My heart beats faster. It happens so close to me, as if I'm with them behind the wall.

They continue to engage in wild love for twenty minutes. Act of complete freedom, breaking all the threads of the normal. They are a threesome, in freedom and pleasure. They live and breathe each other. They exist in this desire. She suddenly begins to moan louder. What a beautiful flight, my heart opened. My wife turns to me and says, "Our neighbor, she is such a whore."

Beautiful and flawless

Beautiful and flawless
Creation of the gods perhaps
As if they sculpted her for themselves
To run their tongues
Up and down her naval bronze.

Performance

I liked the way the clouds performed for us that day
In the place where no man can remain
While I conquered the mountain tops
You let your tears fall without a sound

We stopped in the ancient woods for a night
I recited few lines over the flaming light
While we waited for bears and mountain priests
We stared at the fire and lived in the breeze

Yeah we had a perfect time without calamities
no food,
no mercy,
no idols,
and no vanity

Fire Dance

We gathered here in the woods
To praise the light of day
To swim in the mountain rivers
and to worship the night
and its mystical powers

We gathered here to
 play an ancient tribal drum
to which the forest sways
and unveils before our eyes
the true power that rules our world
and conquers kingdoms
 the magic of the
women dancing around the fire

Fire ablaze and kind, warm land
Circle of strangers and future friends
a Shaman woman sat down with a native drum
and started to sing about a river Volga
that runs through her heart

Calm voice sang
and the mountains held their breath
Walked out
3 dancing silhouettes
light raven hair
bare feet and
white dresses and river eyes

We kept on banging on an ancient drum
we didn't think
we just breathed
we were bound by our eyes
by our fate
by our burning hearts

from under their dress
descended on us
maternal power of the unborn
their bodies swaying in the wind
but they gazed ahead

I fell in love
I wanted to live forever in this moment
between the past and future
It's the closest I ever felt
to my forest gods

Music died down
I closed my eyes, but
the dance never stopped
and every day
it continues in my mind,
in my eyes and ears
the shuffling of the white dress
bare feet
and the river eyes
I wanted to marry one of the
river nymphs

and burn
a map into my heart
back to this circle of love
Out of bounds,
Out of time,
Out of space

But she said it was all an illusion
and I shouldn't draw any conclusions,
since we were all flying high up in the sky
being part of the milky way that night

ABSTRACT

MINUETS

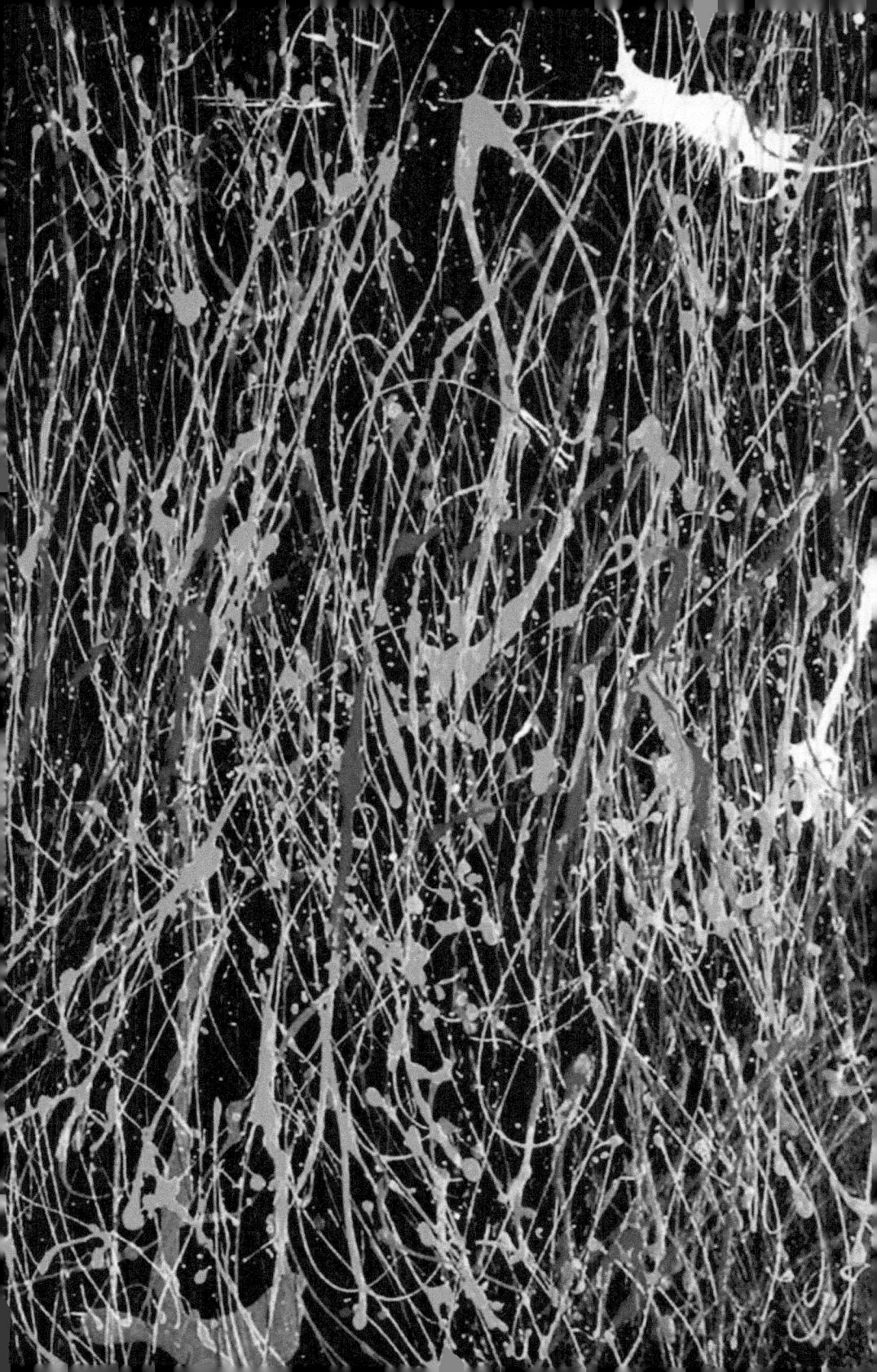

Sometimes we get so caught up in focusing and the next step, the next big thing, the job, the heavy stuff, but life is simple really and there is so much going on all around us.

Let's talk about the silly things. The tiny things, the invisible beautiful things, the glue in between the phrases, mornings and evenings.

It just depends whose eyes are you looking at the world around you with?

If we just let ourselves go and forget our own self-importance and follow some strange silly thought, a road, a path that will take us to a new and unfamiliar place we will realize that something deep within us is constantly trying to tap on our shoulder and make us remember what is it all about.

Arcade

I am in heaven by the sea
somewhere in California

Down by San Francisco Bay
Pier 27 they say

The sea spreads it's legs open
beneath my feet

Fishermen are selling crabs
Like lollypops on sticks

I walk inside an old arcade,
a whole world of forgotten smells

Metal boxer's hands reach out
for a wrestling match

Big slogans in old type script
Binoculars atop of wooden box

Peeping Tom show for the sailors
"Come on in! Come on in!"

The dancing marionette
will raise her dress

Old train cars and circus clowns
"Grab a hammer and test your strength"

Mechanic animals going around
"Drop a nickel mister and I will play,"
said a little penguin sitting on top of
an old wooden train

I want to stay here and
drown in this sweet old time,
but the future calls on my cellphone
I walk outside

Bye old world,
I will return
Perhaps, when I grow
 a little older

Cereal Box

Henry the 8th is really a cat
Wearing a marquise dress and a gold hat

And the moon has an amazing smile
Every time I look up for some time

One of us touches her chocolate neck
Hence I never know which one I am

Carnival sounds and carnival songs
Why worry yourself when you are a gnome

Winged nymph is dancing on top
Bursting fountain of sound

Don't keep your kids off drugs
Let them try it once or twice

Golden Trees

Golden trees staring into the silver water
My eyesight travels without any wings
It's real good to watch the endless clouds
and listen to them tell their history

There is a house of muse and theatre masks
I always like to wander in and sit
The birds, like people live until the dusk
but I just like to close my eyes and live

It's a good day to look around
and to simply want to be
a day like this I'd choose over million of others,
because they live forever in our memory

Morning Chord

When all things fall asleep
I come out and play
I am the one who came
from your dream
I know how to play
while you are asleep
I am the morning chord
I don't know any rules
my notes are all in discord
and to all the sleeping things
I sing my little tune

Alexis

She is 9 years old
She is her parent's china doll

She is spilling all the drinks
Swinging microphone on a silver string

Her sandwiches are 300 dollar worth
But she forgets to make one at all

She's been up since 7 am
She is a rocket in the room

I am playing rock and roll
She is making faces back at me

She says to me,
"We're going to have a race,
but there is one little rule
I always win, but
you always have to loose, ok?"

9 to 5 Ballads

The river is whispering hello
The boat is rushing to the shore
The buildings silently observe
The flapping of the wings of birds

The clocks are falling to the right
The people slide on pavement light
The silent magic of the breeze
The spell is broken I retrieve

Coder

I am a coder
I live in my code
I am a problem
I love to be solved

I love for and while loops
I love conditional clause

If
you love me
Then
everything is good
Else
I will go and love someone else

When my code
gives me errors
I drink and I curse
I get real mean
like Bukowski
I fight with the world

But when it works
I feel as if I smoked some dope
I moan, "That felt good.
Give me more!
Give me more!"

I am still coding
When I am in deep my dreams
I am still coding when I sleep
and I scream,
"Close that bracket."

One time I told my lady
after a passionate kiss,
"Honey you look so good
Why don't you scroll down?"

Co-Worker Alice

Alice in Wonderland
Lives in this crazy world
She sits right next to me
and she knows it all

You want to drown in her eyes
you want to swim in them
but if you go, you may not come
home ever again

She thought this was another dream
In which she meets the cat
but I think now she is really lost
'cause I am the Cheshire Cat

...and we never spoke,
  although I wanted to wrap my striped tail around her
  waist and whisper in her ear,
"Which way you should go depends on where you are
  trying to get to, my dear Alice."

Riding Trains

There is a certain charm to riding trains in America. It was called the Rail 300 years ago, the scary rail that would bring people across the continent, where the new race and the new type of people would invade the Native American way of living. Space to think.

Now travelling outside of New York, you get a certain sense for people, for the air, for what they are living through every day. In New York you are too busy making it somewhere with the blindfolds on.

Siting on wooden benches in Philadelphia station you see impressive white columns and marble floors and a sign that says Red Cap Service with hand wagons.

People are walking back and forth, and you could see how they are more settled in their ways, more acceptant of who they are, of their own slavery to the man that pays them the check.

Even the wheelchair is old, with brown leather seats and iron rods. Making you feel certain you will get there.

There is a statue of a man with wings, carrying a tired, overworked man or a dead man up to heavens.

And the railroad schedule changes not digitally, but roller cards are rotating making the sounds of shuffling cards on the table, may be the Satan is playing cards with our fates.

Don't know why I am writing this? I guess I like the feeling of space and travelling and the observer within asked me to write this down.

EXISTENTIAL

WANDERING

I was always obsessed with big questions
since I was a little boy.
Looking up at the sky,
I thought, what is this place?
Where do we live?
If we live on planet earth then
what's beyond our planets?
Our galaxy, right? What's beyond our
galaxies?
What happens when you reach the end of
the galaxy?
Who created it all?
And what or who created it?
Isn't it the everlasting search that moved
our civilization forward?
Isn't wondering created knowledge and
seeking answers for other humans?
Questions were endless and even my father
that always explained everything couldn't
provide the answers. So there, began my
search within oneself for answers.

Snow and Wine

Smooth sailing,
Wishes
desires

Endlessly wandering soul
finds a home

This year
we will follow the roads to the city

This time
we will see the headless riders
on the seas of creation.
No alienation!

Tie a string around my arm and
give me
a fix of snow
to cleanse my soul
to last a year
so I could fulfill the visions
of the powerful
and all mighty magus

Siddhartha become Buddha
A seed becomes a lotus flower
A dog becomes a wolf
A ray of light becomes the light of day

A sperm becomes a child
A string becomes a song
A wheel becomes the road
A word becomes a howl
A spark becomes a fire
A drop becomes a sea
As snow becomes the wine
And stars will be the guides
Planets will be the gifts
The future becomes the present
and my dreams will become me

What about thee?
Thee, who were born to see?
Remember when we were thieves?
Stealing knowledge
one book at a time
one beat for a rhyme
You couldn't hold back
the river of psychic mystics
They read your thoughts
before you were born
because you spilled yourself
in their dreams

Smell the snow!
What does it smell like?
You haven't been born a fish
to have a loss of scent

Feel the breath of fire
on your tongue and overcome
The madness of the haste.
The taste.
The rush.
The accident.
The traffic to make a buck
To pave the way
with gold and glitter of ego over love

Flow on you are crazy
and vibrant soul!
Transform yourself into the womb
and you will be a baby
in virgin's arms
Don't start again the search for love
The search is done, the love is now
You are in arms of snow and wine

At the MET

Written on a plaque at the Metropolitan Museum of
Art in New York next to a peculiar sculpture:

"The younger man just facing life
Has no conception of his oneness with Divine.
But as soon as he realizes his larger part in the   uni-
verse, as soon as his sense of immortality is born, than
he begins to cast off the earthly and reach for the stars."

Two natures of one man:
One on the ground, aging and beaten
A faggot of the earth
In a pose of earthly laziness
Who gave himself and now
reclines and takes it all

The other version of himself:
young baboon, Asian and strong
stands on his chest, erect
and ready to take off
To run, to fight, to struggle
until there is no ground
beneath his feet
His teeth are out and
ready to bite a piece of galaxy at last,
but his own reflection
in iron bronze,
pulls him back down

towards the earth,
and they pull and tug
on each other's destinies

Who will win and who will lose?
The struggle is in shapes,
but the choice is yours!

Nebulas

We are driving through space
All memories fade
Stars are falling on us
Like rain from Nebulas

A man is a black hole
A star is his girl
Chaos grows with time,
If the things are left alone

If the universe had no creator,
then we can't be destroyed
If the universe has a finale
then it's just like our lives.

Dancing apart
Something holds them together

Words

O words!
You are my weapons
and you are my lovers
I caress the air
with your soft
and violent touches

Words, I know so many of you
in different languages
Words are growing on feelings
Words stacking on top of each other

There are ones we use to express pain:
Fuck, Cunt, Asshole, Dick, Obsess, Jealousy

and there are ones to express the wildest dreams:
Everlasting, Bright, Constellation, Magical,
Lucid Dream

and others to describe your partner:
Caress, Lips, Smear, Neck, Breast, Thigh,
Don't Stop

Words, I know so many of you
My friends and my battalions
I rain them on the pages,
notes and screens

They help me stir the ocean
of varied human emotions

Sometimes I use them
to converse in silence
Sometimes in dreams I utter few
and sometimes when I get tired
I speak the words in my native tongue,
the ones I learned from my celestial Mom
Those make me feel intensely:

Что казалось мне палитрой
На самом деле сон
В который Я давно влюблён
и дух мой здесь запечатлён

Words, I splatter them like war paint
on the surface of the world
and when the ship goes down
who will be the one
to save the last word?

What will it be?

Conversation with It

It was a beautiful day
and I decided to not stay in cafeteria
and stop pretending to work, so I took a walk
outside with my coffee and I saw it:

It was in the air.
It was right there.
I closed my eyes and said,
"THANK YOU."

It said, "I made you well."

I said, "You didn't make it easy."

It said, "Easy is boring. You have got to live
through your own trials, otherwise you wouldn't
have figured out half of the things you know now.

I closed my eyes and the shiver went up my spine.

I said, "I think of dying a lot lately, but the point
is that you can't escape destiny so there is no
reason to worry about it, right?"

It answered, "Kind of stupid really."

I continued, "I finished third Arthurian saga by
Mary Stewart, the one about Mordred, Arthur's

evil son. She definitely set it up for us. Everything was going so well and Mordred ended up being a likeable and a virtuous guy. I thought that for the first time Mordred doesn't have to play that role the classic tale assigned to him, but what was I thinking? You can't escape your destiny. He still did what he was supposed to do and still killed his father, Arthur.

I just wondered, how organized everything is, like a carefully set up plan. We are all moving according to some hidden plan. Best not to know the plan, but still we can wonder about it, right?"

Fading laugher and then silence.

Truth

Enter the future with the open wings
you fit for emperors and kings,
but first, make sure of yourself
and then you ask the nameless man

Shaman of the gods is strong
but he can't tell the right from wrong
That which kills life doesn't die
That which gives life doesn't kill

If men are dying freely
for another man
imagine what would they do
for truth?

Eternal Longing

They say,
that a moment of sadness
is longing for God,
then what do you call
eternal sadness?

Is it one poet's bread?
Or does it belong to ones
who are meant to roam
in the vastness of their feelings?

From one extreme onto the next
I fill my heart up to the brim
with laughter, brews and medicines
but in the end, I am left alone
and stillness deep within
like Narcissus,
my eyes are looking at the lake
but they don't see the lake
they miss the lake
they only see oneself

What's there inside?
The inner king?
The temple of sweet emptiness?
What do you call the distance
between the stars?
Are those thoughts wise, or
they are coming from afar?

I hear no sounds
just empty space ahead of me
and water up above
Am I on the sea floor, looking up?
The ship floating on the surface is
like a dream, it floats
without caressing a single wave
What do you call the space between the ship
and a wave? Poet always wonders...

The things I see
sometimes abandon me,
because my soul
leaves me for a while
to roam the desert,
then it returns, and
narrates to me visions
of perfectly still life
without a sound

Yet I observe the things around
I walk ahead
 Into the space
The space within
I release the tension of a clown
I listen to the words
they fall from fingertips
onto the keyboard,
and on the screen
No meaning just to let it go

to poke a hole
inside that vacuum of sadness,
to let it all flow like a river

A little paper boat headlining the
procession of my thoughts
Now I am ok
I can keep going
I can go on
and walk around and
do the deeds and chores
and watch the screens and magazines

I can do this!
I know I am strong
My heart has emptied itself
I feel nothing, and yet,
I am a vessel full of time
I dive inside
The understanding is left behind
I think, therefore I am
I make eternal sound,
"OM!"

There is no reason
for me to hate you,
I love you,
my emptiness inside!

Now is forever

Road is a snake
that crawls on the map
of our acquired wisdom
Pass over the bridge
that leads to your self
into the light blue window

The past tangled up
in headlights behind
The future beyond this windshield
Right now is forever
and this is our life,
the Buddha and Aton believed it

Goddess Temple

Woke up, got up
jumped into a crisp morning
Breath within a breath,
within a breath
Heat up the skin
jump into an ice cold lake

Shake up hot skin
Shake up my soul
Twirled with my eyes closed
like a bearded Sufi
in a white shawl

Blindfolded,
found myself shaking up the sky
a bell somewhere rang
and then a fire pit without the fire
men huddle before a quest

The leader says,
"For those that are gathered here
this moment happens only once,
and will never happen again.
Only once we walk
together to the lake
so pay attention men
to an old woman hiding
between the trees and leaves

Watch out for what she says or does
Read the signs and take her words
 into your heart."

Then we walk and walk
 and find our sticks to help us climb,
 then we stop, drop down
 and close our eyelids for a moment
Inverted souls,
 bird sounds are fleeting songs
 and then something lit up inside

We walked back I see a frog
 and the frog says,
"Once you are on the path,
 there are no more choices.
The only choice you make is,
 do you want to stay on the path,
 or you want wobble in and out... "
Butterfly comes into my view
 and then she is gone,
 but who was he?
A frog, the wind or
 a teacher with water in his eyes?
Who cares?
It's not a question of who,
 but what did he say?

We make it back...
I hold it in.

Sleep deprecating
Voice rises somewhere within,
"Take me to bed..."

Then, awake again
huddled together again
We try to be good men,
we sit around the fire
without the fire,
While the leathered bikers
on the chrome steel horses
are raping the mountain air
with the sounds of their masculinity.

Different kind of men than we are
and yet we are all the same..

In groups men grow
alone we go

Then somewhere inside
the fire started again
and music flowed and flowed
Brazilian man grabbed the djembe
and I played my usual improvisation in E,
Nature played along
and fires rose from the ground
to our rhythms

What an intensity?!
The rest is silence.

Photographing the Moment

Oh Life,
How we hang onto you
when your sweet silhouette is about to disappear from
our eyes

Oh Life,
how we yearn for you
when your sweet lips are about to say good bye

Oh Life,
how complicated
we phantom you to be
and we break our backs
building glass castles
at the mercy of your strong winds

Oh Life ,
When you are dancing so close to me,
you are a fair maiden with moist lips
and I feel as if I had drunk with the gods

Oh Time,
what a killer whale you are
swimming slowly underneath and occasionally
 bursting fountains of joy over our foolish heads

Oh Time,
you are such a spy

your silent weapon is a clock
and it subtracts one second at a time

Oh Time,
we love to chase you in the mornings
and then we dread your passing when inside a dream
we're floating

Oh Time,
our only weapon against your grip
is when lovers intertwine
their arms and lips pressed tight
then every second becomes an eternity

Oh Now,
How still you are
I observe your sleeping
and your steady breath
I know that your will
leave this earth soon
so I narrate this photograph
of this one second of our time
together on this earth
to remember this moment forever by

Little Hearts on Papers

People leave their hearts
on little papers
They stuff them inside
a holy triangle
They go back and they
swim inside their closed eyes
Swim swim deeper
and deeper inside

One thought at a time
sway the waves of the mind
The thunder and forgotten wrath
turns into a silent brook
Slowly caressing the
earth it ran through
The heart's full or rivers
but this one is true

Priceless Temple

Heart explodes when your father
cries in front of you
because he forgot self-love
somewhere along the way

Horned head facing the wind
laying on the side, staring at the wall
Naked body with the spirit sitting by the bed
How long do I have?

Singing the song of youth
The eyes are rivers
and his wings are folded
but the dreams awake at night

Entities are teachers' now
Invisible healers bound to earth
to whoever believes in their touch
transparent in form and yet full of soul

Take apart the mind's tower
rebuild the castle of lovers
No gold can replace your body
your priceless temple

MIRROR

REFLECTIONS

Self – reflection,
self – analysis,
self – doubt,
self – search
looking into
an internal mirror and asking,
"What am I?"
"What am I?"
Why am I like this?"

A day without the
birth of creation
is wasted

Look in the mirror my friend
You are wearing computer screens
Shake it off and step into a
 room of ancient sounds

The Brain

I started my new job somewhere deep in the state that likes to work. That's what the plaque says upon entry, "State that works." So I guess it's very fit-ting to go to work in a state that works. On my first day at work, I met some people and they were very nice. They seemed to have a lot of time to talk and discuss every little thing. While they were rattling on about the projects and issues with those projects, I found myself feeling a bit jittery and unable to contain myself or even sit in the same chair for more than 10 minutes. I had to constantly switch my positions and pretend I was listening, but I was confused as to why I felt so jittery. More people came and introduced themselves; we spoke and tried to connect, talk some small talk, compliment each other and so on. Then the nice guy with the big title told me that they would have to move me to the table that all the new people get. I agreed, since it's normal to be a newbie and to be put through all the things that newbies are put through. Bring it on.

My new table was in the middle of the floor. The floor was split up in areas of 8 cubicles section. My new cubicle was the one on the left. Once I arrived at my new chair I was told by the people around me that I wasn't going to last there. They said that usually people sit at that table at most for 2 months and then get moved. I wasn't surprised since at my last job I heard the same thing, and the job before that one, so I wasn't new at being new. Still I was perceiving curious coincidences and warnings. People would ask me how I felt at my new spot. I would say , "Ok, I guess."

The next day my jitters increased to a point where I couldn't' even sit in my own chair. I had to move around and would only feel better outside. I would talk to people and want to jump out of my skin. I didn't understand what could be causing such a disturbance. One time I even had to go home since I thought I was going to faint. I thought I was going insane, but next day I went back, vowing to find out what was causing me to feel this way. I am very open to people's energies and receptive to all kinds of things, and can make friends with all sorts of people, but this feeling was something new.

One day I stood up and saw that in the cubicle in front of me a big brain was sitting in the chair. It was big, slimy and the size of a human being, but it was a brain. It was sitting there in a big chair and in front of the brain was a computer. The brain had no arms or legs; it would control and manipulate the computer without doing anything. I was surprised, doesn't anybody else see that there is a brain the size of a human being sitting in the chair, but no, people would walk around and go about their business pretending to not notice anything. Some people would come up and say, "Thank you very much, brain, for your help," or, "It's a pleasure working with you, brain." The Brain in response would just snort or speak softly and keep on explaining something brainy to somebody. The brain talked it's own language. Only the chosen few would understand. The brain had disciples as well, who would sit and listen to what it had to say and the brain would glow and educate them by giving references to books and documents, similar to the way Buddha would educate his disciples under a big Bodhi tree. The only difference was that drops of slime would fall on the floor when the brain talked. I wasn't sure if I liked the brain or not.

My relationship with my own brain was rather strange and difficult. I acquired mine from my mother and father who had theirs working overtime, causing turbulent situations in our lives. I spent my youth doing pranks that my brain told me to do and then in my adulthood I spent a lot of time trying to heal the effects of those pranks. My brain wasn't something I was trying to grow - more like keep it well-groomed and properly fed.

The brain at my work was different. It was in the middle of the room, so there would be brain waves coming out of it left and right. One morning I felt tingles as I walked in the room, my brain started tingling and pulsating as I walked closer. I took a step back and the tingling stopped. I took a step forward and my brain started tingling and pulsating again. I was stunned at the power that brain had. It spanned through the whole floor.

I decided not to despair and I started enjoying my own brain pulsating and growing. When I went to a grocery store I made a new choice. I bought Smart Water thinking that now since my brain was growing I should start drinking Smart Water. I bought a fancy bag that made me look smarter and started dressing sharper and that made me look smarter.

It was one day before Halloween and I was working on some design and I asked another designer a question about font sizes. Since the designer didn't know, she went to ask the brain. The brain spoke softly explaining the solution to the designer. The designer turned to me and said, "You should listen to what the brain is saying." I stood up and saw that the brain was wearing plastic devil horns as a costume. I thought to myself, "what a predicament." Brain was proud of its own understanding of how all things work. As the brain was speaking, I felt insane tingling and sensation in my own brain. I decided to show off my newly acquired brainpower proposing some of my own discoveries about the font sizes, but the brain didn't like that and started replying back to me in a hasty tone. Brain even got a tiny bit hostile at my disrespect and turned a bit yellow! It expressed the wish and will to be respected and admired by all. After the brain was done talking I didn't have anything to say, so I just said, "Ok cool," and sat down. The designer, not knowing what to say next, replied, "Well, there's your answer." The brain's color subsided from yellow back to pink, got moist, and went back to it's normal mode of explaining something brainy to someone else close by.

I went to the restroom, washed my face and looked at myself in the mirror. I saw that my own head had grown 3 times the size it used to be. I was scared I didn't know what to do with my new enlarged brain.

Next day was Halloween, so I wore a Wizard hat with stars on it to show the brain that magic is part of life, too. I went to work walking tall and proud, but the brain didn't show up to work and I had the best brainless day.

Artistic Contemplation

I am sitting here
A man of statue and a pose
Good heart and a
loud belly laugh

I am a man
That had felt things
And felt them deep in his soul

A man that had loved strong
and has been loved before
A man who could see far and clear
And yet can stumble upon a simple tear

when he hears a lovely voice
or people dancing in joy
or actors falling in love

or see such colors that rumble his insides
or a sweet song in tune with time
And yet he still doesn't know which
hearts expression he should pursue?
What castle should he storm?

Oh help me words,
My ravens from inside!
I beg you show me the light,

My tunnel is dim
My words take flight!

My plight is thus:
I am filled with passion for the acting art
When life is acted out through
other people's hearts

I feel so moved by a well-spoken line,
a gesture, a word, a scene or the obscene
a purity of acting is in the
transparency of actor's soul

He or she stands there
above the crowd and speaks aloud
with a vivid imagination of another lover,
seeker, fighter or a thief
reenacting the life of foes, friends or
lovers in the night
struggling to savor the lost passion
but actor is a thief of life!

He steals life from the characters he plays
I too am an actor in my prime
I am acting out this life of mine
splattered on canvas
with some red paint

Oh the Paints!

I feel immense pleasure
feeling the colors in my hands
As if a young boy's erect penis enters
soft vagina for the first time

He is overfilled with joy and
an immense desire to release the fill
onto the canvas as I have spilled
my thoughts and feelings Like a God,

I would paint mountains
eyes, stars, and comets all with one streak
since I never learned to draw

At my command they would splatter
and splash upon the canvas
and I would cry out in ecstasy.
when I touched the yellow;
Sun was shining in my soul
When I used blue
the heavens opened up for me
and when I got a hold of red,
the passion and the feeling so direct
It made me clench my teeth
and throw more paint
 with long and hungry streaks

It gave me so much pleasure

deep inside and then
I fell exhausted on my bed,
but made a vow that I will do it again,
because the pleasure is immense

And then the sound of music
 filled my ears in the sweet hour of the morning,

Oh music,
So sweet and sour,
so filled with love,
mystery, joy and fear

Those extremities filled my ears
as the sound invaded my entire being

Since I was sixteen I lay there
with a tasty cigarette burning in the dark
and listened to the sounds of the
mystique upon the nightly gloom

And yet, musician is a performer
He stands and plays one note
one gaze, one stare, one motion
and the crowd is on fire

The ancient satyr on hind legs
he leaps with joy strumming his lyre
your soul is lit and
sends a shiver up your spine

You yell:
My love is alive!
I dance, I move, I sing
I teach, I praise, I learn
I play the notes
and yet I am laying still

What a mix of sounds
visual ecstasy
and triumph
of one heart
delivering orgasms
to mind, eye, soul and ear

What a perfection of the moment
listening to the sound of
emotions intertwined with
the embroidery of notes

And then there is the art of
writing down your own thoughts
A language of the sub-conscious mind

I vow to not foretell a lie,
but when we write we think
Do we not?

We think
and we write down the words

as a result of observation
of moments passing in front of our eyes

Our pen uncovering
the secret meaning behind
this life's manuscript
For writing is a skill
To talk on paper silently
with a partner in your head
to explore the universe
within oneself

Narrate events or to
imagine life of fiction
to prove a point or to
prevent a riot in the brain

Oh what an art form it is
Capturing one's thoughts!

The reader gets a glimpse inside
into a world of silent speeches
so he won't have to deal with his
or her present sorrow
or maybe find a companion for the night
a good book will make you feel alive
and yet leave you alone

Oh what an abstract art the writing is?

Therefore, I felt
expressions of all those arts
and understood
we are the means
that spirit uses to reveal itself
and share the gift of being alive
with our peers

You read a word
words make up a song
song is backdrop for a movie
movie is acted out in scenes
by actors reading out their scripts
but, what is a scene?

A scene is a mix of still paintings
with a plot to capture a piece of life
with an intent to make us feel
how souls ignite

Just be thy art, and feel it
speak through you
One at a time, for every day
carries a different song
that you can hear if you can only
listen to its chime

Unanswered Question

Unanswered question still stands,
Music is it the Devil's work?
or
Divine intervention of God?

Silence.

"Perhaps both."

How can it be?

"What blasphemy?" A priest would say.

A high school girl would clasp the latest album closer
to her bosom,
"This is my favorite album," she would whisper in the
night and have impure thoughts with every member of
the band

Writers Plight

Bukowski was a great old crooner
Henry Miller thought that sex was God,
Jack Kerouac thought the road was magic
Henry S. Thompson's thought that drugs were fun
Tolstoy was stuck between the war and peace
Garcia Marques thought solitude was King
Dostoevsky made you get lost
between the right and wrong
While Rumi wrote divine rhymes
Paulo Coelho was a magician with a sword
and I am proud to be walking in their footsteps
with my laptop and hair full of thoughts

Conversation with a Shadow

(Knock! Knock! Knock!)

ME:
Who is there?

SHADOW:
It's your shadow staring at you through the air.

ME:
Hey what's going on?
What's the occasion for such an unexpected invasion?

SHADOW:
Nothing just came to check up on you
to see that all your troubles are through
that your head sits tight,
your eyes see all right or
there is some kind of new despair tonight?

ME:
I was thinking where is it going?
I mean I jumped from the skies,
I fell and I screamed
and then I did a lot of wild things
but anywhere I go,
my sister sadness follows me

The world seems to be fighting
for thousands of years
and nothing changed
It's always for the same reasons
The darkness fighting the light,
while the new world
tries to stand up for its right
evolution hides in the dark
Arrogance is the new Tzar
Muse wears a price tag
and art is nothing more than a
one night stand before the new year

SHADOW:
Hey man, I will tell you this,
in case you lost the string
The world is nothing more
than a boxer's ring
The rules are always the same;
someone will lose and someone will win
So u can't change this world,
don't try that hippie thing
Take your art to the top,
Grab on this silver thread
think of what you want to say,
but quit trying to say something new,
the words are insignificant tools
they have been used and abused
by the millions of fools

So the bottom line is,
nobody knows what art means
The emotions are like rivers in the spring
softly running between stones and leaves
and unless you are a fish, you can't live in the sea
but you are more than a fish
You are an ocean
Where the water, wind, earth, fire and skies
found their own sunrise,

Let your storm settle down,
and you will see the higher ground…
Just move in the direction of your fears,
forget the tears…

Good night,
good night,
Adieu,
until next time,

My young troubled soul
I will be watching you

Age is a Monster

Age is a monster
Age is a beast
It leaves scars on our faces
but guess what?

It's also a wise punk
beaten and bruised
stern and intellectually rude
It knows what works
and what doesn't
It knows who to send to hell
and who to embrace

Age is also child
It makes us cry like a baby
and whine like an old man
who didn't get his newspaper
for breakfast

Age is an experienced slut
It knows how to make you sell
whatever needs to be sold
It knows how to wear wigs and faces
It knows how to turn
into a completely different person
with a snap of our fingers
It knows how to pretend
you are hurt or offended

It knows how to demand
your pay for the time you worked

Age is something to embrace
It's not going away,
except for the hair on our head
they are like the leaves in the fall,
but we can still trim that lawn
in the latest fashion
and we are young again...

THE LIGHT OF
FATHERHOOD

Dar Luz

In Spanish, they call it Dar Luz
Translated to English, "To Give light!"
In Russian, "Dar" means a present

We are all anticipating
the gift from heavens
to be delivered into our lives
It's been almost 9 months,
my favorite number

Why is the waiting season
has 9 in it?
The creator takes 9 months
to work his magic

Where everything has been
well thought off,
the arms,
the legs,
the head,
the bones,
the heart

I saw his heart
Just like a walking drum,
just like the rhythm of planet earth
one second at a time.

Just to think
how many beats are in
9 days,
9 weeks,
9 months,
9 years,
99999999 years

What will it be?
A mix of us
with all our accomplishments,
courage, all our faults, habits and misgivings or
will it be a unique creation of its own
inspired by the Ying and Yang.

Will he change the ebb and flow
of our lives and universe perhaps?
Will it howl loudly at night or
sleep soundly during the day?
Anticipation.

Last few days until the gift of light
is delivered into our lives

Those days are tense,
but the deliverance is near.

Dar Luz is here.

The Birth of a Cub

I yelled out loud,
"My son is home!" -
and threw my hat up in the air three times
It feels as if my heart has been cracked open and the
water has been poured in,
but not the water that you drink,
more like an elixir of life
has been poured over my heart
and now it's in sync
with the beat of planet earth

The planning, the anticipation and the wait
Thousands of words can't describe
how it feels to have your child at home

I am not sure if I should take photos
of his every move and share with everyone I know,
or write thousands of new songs dedicated
to his every crest that I already learned

Few days old and already he shows
traits of character and determination,

What does he cry about?
Does he want food?
Does he want to be hugged?
Does he cry about an incident from a previous life?

He doesn't want to put that shirt on,
or suck on a boob, his demands and cries
sink into our worried hearts
We watch him like the hawks
and already so much has changed

That realization that my love and I
are now forever tied and now
our trees are intertwined
They will grow together
branches helping each other grow,
putting all we have into our little tree,
growing near by

The love like this unfelt before,
even love for a woman is divine,
but this love is a universal kind,
It makes you tremble at his every squawk,
his yells and cries are
like a thousand of knives enter your heart
and you don't know
Why? What and How?
since he can't talk,
so you just stand there and
guess, may be this?
or may be that?

My god, you have never warned me
of this love before,

I have not had the anticipation or the skills
to open to such knowledge of this earth

One thing is clear,
I am at peace with the world and with myself
I find this planet to be a warm place now
I want to live and raise my contribution
to this wild world

I walk down the streets now quietly
and my soft steps are heard a mile away since the
silence has descended into my being

Wait, my cub is yelling out
into this world
Silence and peace are
broken once again
He is dissatisfied with the world
and why is he not fed yet?!

Expectations

Don't expect everything
to be perfect

Expecting it to be perfect is
like watching a chick try to fly

If on the first time it doesn't happen
Does it give up?
No, it keeps on trying

Don't expect your baby to
find a tit to suck on right away
and know that food comes from sucking it?

Don't expect a child to learn how to speak
Don't expect a youth to learn how to find friends
Don't expect a teenager to learn how to love
The human beings have survived because of their abil-
ity to keep on trying and adapting

Why does your mind keep on
foreseeing the worst possible future?
Do you not deserve a better one?
Do you not trust in the hands above helping you?
Do you not trust in the order
of everything working out in the universe?
Why do you sink in fear?
Is your fear stronger than your fate?

No, say onto your ego!
Don't foresee the worst possible
future, don't you dare!
You deserve the best possible outcome

My faith is bigger than the fear!
I trust in the universe and
don't expect the worst,
but only the best from it

Say it,
"I now let go of fear and control
Everything is working out for the best of all."

Why?
Because I said so!
Who is I?
I, is the one that created you
that is writing this

I gave you light,
I gave you arms and legs
I made you survive many diseases,
the breaking bones,
the first heartbreak,
and the first nosebleed
Therefore trust in me
and don't trust in doubt

Doubt is created by your mind.
Train the mind to think otherwise
in the hardest situations and
the light will shine forth
and if doubt enters you again,
look at yourself in the mirror,
look at your limbs and face,
and strong legs and strong arms and say,
"I trust in what I see before me,
therefore I trust in creator
helping everything under its light."

Now close your eyes and go to sleep.
«Утро вечера мудренее»
(The morning is wiser than the evening)
Old Russian Proverb.

Beyond Awesome

She is like a panther with her triapo
(Triapo in spanish, is a cloth for wiping dirt)
only this triapo is for wiping drool
from baby's mouth

She leans closer to the ground
and springs forward
catching the spit as it
descends from our son's mouth

This panther is a mother
and my wife
Throughout the day
she must have wiped his mouth
a thousand times with words
"Babychini how can you drool so much?"

He squawks and with a look of serious determination
let's out another waterfall of saliva
right on his newly
changed shirt, but she is ready
She wipes again

Then he farts and a diaper
is full of bodily fluids.
He looks innocent and quiet
She exclaims,

"Babychinni you pooped again?"
Change of a diaper

Then the cries of sleepiness
and he can't fall asleep without
his mom rocking him to sleep
He is finally asleep
Oh, the silence! Oh, the freedom!
She runs and catches up
with all her friends.
She checks her mail
She thinks of all the things
that are left undone
Leftovers of a dream,
she starts writing quick.
He is up.

1 hour passed like 5 minutes.
He is hungry now.
She watches for that moment
when he is smacking on his lips
She takes out her weapons
Her bosoms full of milk
and sticks a boob
right in his mouth

He yanks it and pulls away
then sucks a bit
then complains then yanks

then restless. She talks to him and
he agrees the he should eat and then
he is calmly drinking for a bit

Then once he is done
the burp is what we seek the most
If he didn't burp, then
all kinds of troubles
will be born
and more cries

Ahhh, the burp is here
We all clap
Relief
We saved ourselves
Then he is happy again
and hanging off of her shoulder
staring at the world
showering us with smiles
that outweigh the gold
and then, all of a sudden
puke and on her new shirt

She wipes exclaiming,
"Babychinni I just changed this shirt!"
He smiles. She smiles back and changes her shirt quick
and then again the drool is coming on.
and this circle of life happens
every 2 hours through-out the day

Dishes are unwashed
The house is a mess
Clothes are everywhere
The bibs and children's
clothes are in my chair

Then she cries to me at night
She is exhausted
She is beyond tired
She feels like she loses herself
The motherhood is taking over
like a white veil
She feels like she is a horrible mother

I tell her you are beyond awesome.

Father and his Monster

Parenthood is not a fair game. It's an investment into a brighter future, I think that's the correct way of saying it. Parenthood is against everything we have been raised to be, the "give me everything now" mentality. Parenthood is about perseverance, it's about the long haul, it's about stamina.

I wanted kids all my life. I knew I was going to be a father. My father set a great example for me, and I knew one day I would be one. It was just a matter of when and with whom. It happened finally 2 years ago.

And now…

His first word, or the powerful meaning of the sound, "No!" drives you up the wall. He starts using that as a reply to everything you ask him.

"Do you want this?" – "No."
"Do you want that?" – "No."
"Do you want to eat?" – "No."
"Do you want to go outside?" – "No.".

It's absolute worst when your baby has been sick for a week with a fever. You prepare for him all the foods he's used to eating, and when the most important thing for him is to eat, he says, "No," and turns away crying.
He wakes up at least twice or thrice during the night. He

scowls and whines if you turn away to sleep. At night we have to play with toys. Kid I gotta go to work. He cries. "Choo Choo Train!" You say fine, let's go "Choo Choo Train!" He doesn't want to eat the food that you prepared for him, but at daycare he eats perfectly. The day care teacher says he is the best kid on the planet. He eats everything and she sends you photos of him laughing and playing with the other kids. You start thinking where did I go wrong? Maybe I am giving off a repulsive scent that only he can smell and his appetite turns sour, along with his mood. At times, you feel like you are in cage or a jail cell and you can't leave. You have to stay. It's like a hangover that doesn't end. At least when you're hungover you know that no matter how bad it is, it will end at some point and you will feel better. The difference with parenthood is that you don't know when and if it ever will change from the way you feel right now.

Different people say different things; they say it never changes. They say they never grow up so you always worry about them. Maybe they are right, you never really relax and take a deep breath unless you are at the beach somewhere and even then you worry about something or someone jumping out of the water eating or stealing your baby. It's a crazy feeling.

When I work freelance jobs and someone asks that I work more than agreed, they can forget it. On the rare occasion that I can do it, I will justify it with a nice invoice, including a nice fat extra charge on top, and I will go to sleep soundly. Here with baby you don't get paid. You don't get vacations.

You don't get weekends. You are trying to live in between those scowls, whines, constant cries and sobs.

Me and my wife took a trip to Florida for a few days. You are lying in bed and you get up stretching, telling your wife, "Wow, we are in Florida." You arranged everything for someone to take care of your kid back home. It's beautiful and sunny out and we can go sit at the beach and get some drinks. Come on let's go, we are finally alone together." Your wife turns to you and says, "I am not going anywhere. I am sleeping in this white bed." All of a sudden you realize you haven't slept for two years and you say, "Fuck it! You are right, this bed is the best thing I have seen since I bought my last guitar," and you go back to bed, and you sink into the deepest sleep of your life.

What's surprising is that you have millions of ideas about starting a new business, new project, writing new music, finishing old projects. Building plans and solutions in your head sounds perfect. All you need is to just go and do it, and you are stuck sitting at the playground concerned that your precious baby will fall off the slide and you run and save him and those projects / ideas / solutions are gone, and by the time you come back to sit at that same bench you already forgot what you were thinking about and you are pissed because your projects don't get done and the dishes are unwashed and you are perpetually fucking exhausted and you get up and go to work. Your friend says, "Dude you don't look too good. Did you sleep ok?" and your co-worker says, "My god, I couldn't sleep well last night. I went to this new Indian restaurant with my boyfriend and the food was weird. I got up at 8am, imagine." You just roll your eyes, and try not to yell profanities at her, since your get up hours are 2am, 4am and 5:30am is the hour to start your day, no matter when you went to sleep the night before.

As you sit there propped against the wall at 6am in the kid's room feeling sorry for yourself, asking yourself, "Why me? Why did I create this? I fucked up really bad. Now my life is over." Then you are feeling even more miserable for feeling sorry for yourself and then while you drown in self-pity and confusion the little monster turns around and says your name. He says your name in a way only your dearest mother or your wife say. Your wall of misery and self-inflicted pain collapses in a second and your eyes get watery and you say, "Ah you little one, stop making me cry over here," and you go and hug him real hard. Then he yells, "Boogers!" or "Water!" or "Toys." He doesn't really call you to say, "Thanks for everything Papa. I am sorry," – No, he just wants to get your attention so you could give him something, but that way he said your name stays with you. It sinks deep, really deep and you are going to live with that way he said your name for the rest of your life and your heart opens a little bit more, and you're thinking, it's ok. I can do this. This will pass. He will grow up one day and we can finally talk. I can tell him what I found out about this life. May be he will even read this story and decide to write a story of his own.

To my little son, Wolfe.
—July 2016

Brooklyn Mornings

I remember waking up in Brooklyn
in your cozy little room
David Bowie playing on a stereo
Hung-over from the night before

Aimlessly roaming the city
we were looking for something,
but we didn't notice
we have found each other already

Waking up next to long and exotic you
waking up next to my future in your bed
You, luscious mysterious and strong
You would make a good mother; I think to myself

Now we are sitting on a wooden floor
and we gave birth to the new me and you
We have grown into parents,
but the same music still
plays on my speakers
conjuring up the same feelings

Hung-over happiness
and loose mornings with you
are the best way to spend my life

2nd Shooting Star

Just as we thought there is not enough
 joy and silent music in this world,
the 2nd shooting star landed into our arms
and we forgot how perfect can simple moment be
How can life be filled with so much
perfection and tranquil peace
when we put this little star to sleep

In the morning he fills the room with rays of light
and when star looks at you it warms your heart
You forgot what? Why and how? and exclaim,
"Just let me hold this little star a bit longer"
In the evening he smiles again, "Bye, see you soon!"

I never knew that a little star could be sleeping
in the crib so close to us and makes us recreate
the start of life again
while clock hands are ticking away
we wish upon a star!

Hand from Above

I know we had our
disagreements
about trivial matters
of whether to sing or to get paid

Especially I miss the times
when we would sit
with our fishing rods
in an old wooden boat
in the middle of the lake
and we would ask the
gods of the lake
to send us few of
their sons and daughters
and he listened to our prayer
and we would catch so much fish that day

Now all I can say is this,
"So many times I feel
your hand reached out from above
to help me in the time of most need
and for that I want to THANK YOU!"

Although, my heart pains
from the fact that
you will never meet your grandsons,
but he will know you through us
because you live in all your children

Your light lives on!

I got nothing to complain about
Such is the contract we all sign
when we come to planet earth
We come and go
What's done is done
When it's your time to live you live
When it's your time to go you go
Jim was right,
"No one gets out of here alive!"

www.ingramcontent.com/pod-product-compliance
Lightning Source LLC
LaVergne TN
LVHW051057080426
835508LV00019B/1935